Pocket

Christmas

Pocket
Christmas

compiled by
Nick and Hazel Whitehead

National Society/Church House Publishing

National Society/Church House Publishing
Church House
Great Smith Street
London
SW1P 3NZ

ISBN 0 7151 4844 3

First published in 1995 by The National Society and
Church House Publishing

Cover design and illustration by Julian Smith
Text design and typesetting by The National Society

Printed in England at the University Printing House,
Cambridge

Contents

Dedicated to
Andrew, Matthew and Jonathan

Introduction

Of all the seasons in the year, it is Christmas which evokes the strongest feelings in people of all ages – whether that be the excitement of the small child on Christmas Eve, the stress of prolonged entertaining or the apprehension of those for whom Christmas Day will be a difficult or lonely time.

The biblical story of the birth of Christ in the manger surrounded by shepherds, kings, and angels is complemented in this book by a wealth of modern pieces, all of which have the meaning of Christmas at the centre.

A lot of material from this book has been used already in worship and it is hoped that it will be a valuable resource for other churches and schools, as well as being helpful to families and individuals.

Advent

L ord, as we prepare for Christmas, may the
    Advent candles remind us of your light, your
peace, your joy and your love.

Advent

A s we enter, eager and expectant, into this solemn season of Advent, looking forward to the birth of the Christ child, let us renew in ourselves that vision of God's perfect kingdom which is the end of all our strivings and the consummation of God's loving purposes for us.

In sorrow and penitence we confess our failures and shortcomings, and seek pardon for those sins which frustrate his redemptive purposes and hinder the advent of his reign of love.

So in prayer, praise, and song do we give voice to the hope set forth in the Scriptures, that his kingdom shall come; and, as we prepare for that day to dawn upon us from on high, so we commend ourselves and the whole human family to his keeping.

May he guide us into the way of peace, give light to those who sit in darkness and the shadow of death, and kindle in us the fire of his love.

Amen. Come, Lord Jesus.

The Promise of His Glory

No Waiting

There is no Advent in this world
Whatever the Church lectionary might say.
The world does not understand Advent
It cannot wait; it does not want to wait;
It has lost the art. It wants things now.
It cannot wait for anything but grabs it while it can
before it is too late.
Too late for what?

For without the waiting
There will be no Coming
And without the Coming
There will be no meeting
And without the meeting
God and Man will not be one.

Hazel Whitehead

Advent

Advent wreaths are used in many Christian churches to symbolise the waiting time of Advent and the eager anticipation of Christmas. There are five candles, though traditions vary about the colours they should be and their significance. The simplest suggestion is that one candle is lit on each Sunday in Advent and the central, white candle on Christmas Day to show that Jesus has been born.

Other traditions give greater meanings to the four candles and say that the first one represents the patriarchs – Abraham, Isaac and so on, through whom God spoke to Israel; the second is for the prophets – Elijah, Isaiah, Jeremiah, etc. The third is for John the Baptist, the forerunner of Christ and the one who announced his imminent arrival; the fourth is for the Virgin Mary, who accepted God's task for her, readily and willingly, thus contributing in a not insignificant way to God's work. The Advent prayers and collects reflect these themes. Most important, though, is the lighting of the white or gold candle for Christ – the long-awaited One.

The Collect for Advent Sunday

Almighty God,
give us grace to cast away the works of
   darkness
and to put on the armour of light,
now in the time of this mortal life,
in which your Son Jesus Christ came to us in great
   humility;
so that on the last day,
when he shall come again in his glorious majesty to
   judge the living and the dead,
we may rise to the life immortal;
through him who is alive and reigns
   with you and the Holy Spirit,
one God, now and forever. Amen.

Alternative Service Book, 1980

Eternal God,
you have warned us
that your Son the Bridegroom will come at midnight,
at an hour when we are least aware.
Let's ever hear the cry,
'The bridegroom is coming',
so that we may never be unprepared to meet him,
our Lord and Saviour Jesus Christ.

Lancelot Andrewes

Come, Lord Jesus, do not delay;
give new courage to your people
who trust in your love.
By your coming, raise us
to the joy of your kingdom,
where you live and reign
with the Father and the Spirit,
one God for ever and ever. Amen.

The Promise of His Glory

Around the manger

Lord, let us journey to Bethlehem as those who knelt before you on the first Christmas Day.

Around the manger

Wonderful, wonderful in the sight of angels
A great wonder in the eyes of faith.
To see the giver of being,
the generous sustainer
and ruler of all things
in the manger, in swaddling clothes
and without a place to lay his head.
And yet the bright host of glory
worshipping him now.

Canon A Allchin

Incarnatus Est

Glory to God on earth peace
Let this song never cease.

As I arise this morn
Christ in me be born

When I wash my face
Bless me with your grace

When I comb my hair
Keep me from despair

When I put on my clothes
Your presence Lord disclose

This is the day that you are born
Let every day be a Christmas morn

Glory to God on earth peace
Let this song never cease.

David Adam

Around the manger ————————

A Prayer for the Christmas Crib

As children of God
and followers of the Lord Jesus,
we ask for God's blessing on this Christmas crib.
We pray that all who come into this church may stop
and wait and look within
to wonder that God should choose such a place to be
born.
Bless those who come, like the wise men, with riches
and gold to offer;
bless those who come, like the shepherds, with little
to give but their hearts;
bless mothers and fathers and help them to be, like
Mary and Joseph, obedient and true
But most of all, bless the children
wide-eyed and eager, cheeky and chirpy,
smiling and innocent, sticky and squirmy.
Bless them all, both friend and stranger
that they may worship God in the manger.

Hazel Whitehead

Whatever gifts God bestowed on us
    There was no one who could
Understand true love
Until Mary, in her goodness,
And with deep humility,
Received the gift of Love,
She it was who tamed wild Love
And gave us a lamb for a lion;
Through her a light shone in the darkness
That had endured so long.

Hadewijch of Brabant

Mary

Mary will have her own place in your life.
You cannot separate her from the Lord
who chose her as His mother and His bride.

She is the selfless space
where God became man;
she is the silence in which God's Word can be heard.
She is the free woman, subject to none,
not even to the powers of evil.

She is the image of the Church.
Her self-effacing service will guide you to the Lord.
Her faith and fidelity
are a model for your life.
She has trodden all the paths
of our human existence;
she has gone through darkness and suffering, through
the abyss of loneliness and pain.

She is the little creature
through whom God's grandeur shines out;
she is the poor one filled
with divine riches.
She is wholly grace
and grace for you.

Then take your part joyfully
in the prophecy of scripture:
'Behold, henceforth, all generations
will call me blessed.'

Benedictine Priory 'Regina Pacis'

I saw a stable, low and very bare
A little child in a manger.
The oxen knew Him, had Him in their care,
To men He was a stranger.
The safety of the world was lying there,
And the world's danger.

Mary Elizabeth Coleridge

Around the manger ———————

Y ou are the radiant white lily
   Whom God perceived
Prior to all creation.
You the most beautiful and loveliest;
God so delighted in you that he pressed within you
The passionate embrace of his own heat,
So that his own son was suckled by you.
Truly has your body contained joy,
Since out of you every heavenly harmony sounded,
Because Virgin you carried the Son of God,
When your own purity became illuminated in God.

Hildegard of Bingen

The circle of a girl's arms
have changed the world
the round and sorrowful world
to a cradle for God.
She has laid love in his cradle.
In every cot, Mary has laid her child.
In each comes Christ.
In each Christ comes to birth,
comes Christ from the Mother's breast,
as the bird from the sun returning,
returning again to the tree he knows
and the nest to last year's rifled nest.
Into our hands
Mary has given her child,
heir to the world's tears,
heir to the world's toil,
heir to the world's scars,
heir to the chill dawn
over the ruin of wars.
She has laid love in his cradle
answering for us all.
'Be it done unto me'

Caryll Houselander

A Reluctant Joseph

Try as I might I could not convince him that playing Joseph was a great honour. 'Lots of little boys would love to be Joseph,' I encouraged.

'I wanted to be a soldier and carry a sword.'
'I don't think there are any soldiers in a nativity play, are there?'
'There are in this one. And they get to wear silver armour. I have to have a stupid tea towel tied round my head with string. I'll look really stupid. And I have to put my arm round Jessica Brown and the other boys will say I love her and I DON'T!'

Keeping an arm's length between him and the dreaded Jessica and with not the flicker of a smile, he did it, tea towel and all. 'Doing the things you don't really want to do is what makes a man of you' I told him. 'I'm proud of you. We could hear every word and you didn't forget a line.' He grunted. The ordeal was over, thank the Lord. But I wondered whether the real Joseph had been as reluctant to play his part in the first Nativity.

Hazel Whitehead

No room at the inn, no room anywhere.
They gave him the only place they could spare
and the promised Messiah was born that night
on the floor of a stable without any light
where they cut the cord and cleaned up the mess
and wrapped him in somebody's workaday dress
and while Mary slept there, exhausted and cold,
Joseph sat by feeling helpless and old.
This wasn't the way he had thought it would be
when the angel had told him that destiny
chose them to look after the Holy One.
No, this was a farce. What God had done
was to trust the care of the saviour instead
to a man who could not even find him a bed,
and his anger grew hot when the shepherds burst in
all breathless and wild
and stopped in their tracks when they saw the child.
They shifted their gaze from the baby's bed
and their eyes met his and he nodded his head
standing awkwardly, not knowing quite what to do
now they all knew for certain the story was true.

Godfrey Rust

Around the manger

What shall we offer thee, O Christ,
Who for our sakes hast appeared on earth as a
man?
Every creature made by thee offers thanks.
The angels offer thee a hymn;
The heavens, a star;
The magi, gifts;
The shepherds, their wonder;
The earth, its cave;
The wilderness, the manger;
And we offer thee a Virgin Mother.
O God from everlasting, have mercy upon us.

Eastern Orthodox Rite

Come and with divine songs let us also go to
meet Christ and let us receive him whose
salvation Simeon saw. This is he whom David
announced: this is he whose words the prophets
uttered, who for our sakes has taken flesh and
speaks to us in the law. Let us worship him.

Orthodox Rite

At the Inn

'Go away,' said the man
    At the door of the inn,
'Go away and try some other place,
I've no room and I'm tired
And there's work to be done
 And I've just filled the last space.'
'You may stay,' said the man
At the door of the inn,
'In that stable 'til morning at least.
You may sleep there, I'll bring you
Some food and some cloaks
There's no light but that star in the east.'

And many a time in the years that went past,
The innkeeper would stand at his door,
And think of the night that he nearly said 'no'
To the two but requesting a floor.
And he'd look at the stable and look at the stars
And wonder at every thing,
The mother and father, the shepherds and star
And the babe that was born to be King.

Neil Connell

Manger

It happened as had been told.
It could not have been otherwise.
'Lying in a manger' the voice had said.
Mangers were familiar to us.
We had watched as boys
The carpenter shaping, smoothing
The stubborn wood. Here
We were at home
Among the things we understood.
Lying in a manger he was.
His face wrinkled like that
Of my own son. Hurtling
From terror to tenderness,
From angel song to baby's crying,
I touched the strong wood,
Needing reassurance in a night
That had suddenly broken asunder
With the full glory of day.

Sheila Reid

The Shepherd's Journey

For us it was but a short journey
down our familiar hill,
past landmarks we had always known.
We should not have been
surprised by the angels –
we had always sensed their presence;
known, especially at lambing,
and when the snows melt up in the hills,
and new blades of green thrust upward.
God is born in every living thing –
this special babe was something we understood.
That God should choose this way
lit up the dark with glory –
the silence of the stars bursting with song.
What was it, peace to men of goodwill?
Yes, for us it was a simple journey;
only the wise have far to travel.

Cecily Taylor

The Bethlehem Star

Moonless darkness stands between.
Past, the Past no more be seen!
But the Bethlehem star may lead me
To the sight of him who freed me
From the self that I have been.
Make me pure, Lord; thou art holy;
Make me meek, Lord; thou wert lowly;
Now beginning, and alway;
Now begin, on Christmas day.

Gerald Manley Hopkins

O God our loving father,
help us rightly to remember the birth of Jesus
that we may share in the songs of angels,
the gladness of the shepherds
and the worship of the wise men.
May the Christmas morning
make us happy to be your children,
and the Christmas evenings
bring us to our beds with grateful thoughts,
forgiving and forgiven, for Jesus' sake. Amen.

Robert Louis Stevenson

God our Father,
the angel Gabriel told the Virgin Mary
that she was to be the mother of your Son.
Though Mary was afraid,
she responded to your call with joy.
Help us, whom you call to serve you,
to share like her in your great work
of bringing to our world your love and healing.
We ask this through Jesus Christ,
the Light who is coming into the world. Amen.

The Promise of His Glory

Send us an angel

L ord God: some of us are a little like the
   Shepherds:
just carrying on with our jobs . . . despite the
turbulence in the world scene.
Give us a message . . . send us an angel
that will start us seeking a new way of life.

Lord God: others of us are like the Wise Men from
   the east;
we can see the need of some power to come and to
   give us direction:
but we don't know in which direction to go.
Give us the wisdom to see that it is not in
physical power that our salvation lies
but in love and humility.

Lord God: a few of us are like Herod;
we don't want a new power to enter the world,
in case it might threaten our own power.
Give us the humility to be ready
for quite a new form of power;
to fit the dangerous age in which we live;
where atomic power is beyond our capacity to
   control.

We ask you to make us expectant,
 instead of planners;
We ask you to make us seekers,
rather than know-alls.

We ask you for grace
so that we are ready to receive.
We ask you for humility
so that we are prepared to accept your way of doing
    things.
We ask you for faith and faith is a gift, really to
    believe;
that in this dark day for our land, we can accept the
    gift of Christmas:
and bring our wealth as a land to serve the Christ;
to bring our incense to worship Him:
and our myrrh, the symbol of burial,
to be ready to die for Him.
Thus shall we be able
to receive the gift of love and light and life,
when Christmas Day shall dawn.

George MacLeod

Around the manger _____

Collect for Christmas Day

Almighty God, who hast given us thy only-begotten Son to take our nature upon him, and as at this time to be born of a pure Virgin; Grant that we being regenerate, and made thy children by adoption and grace, may daily be renewed by thy Holy Spirit; through the same our Lord Jesus Christ, who liveth and reigneth with thee and the same Spirit, ever one God, world without end. Amen.

Book of Common Prayer (1928)

Eternal God, who by the shining of a star led the wise men to the worship of your Son: guide by his light the nations of the earth that the whole world may behold your glory; through Jesus Christ our Lord. Amen.

Alternative Service Book (1980)

The Oxen

Christmas Eve, and twelve of the clock.
'Now they are all on their knees,'
An elder said as we sat in a flock
By the embers in hearthside ease.

We pictured the meek, mild creatures where
They dwelt in their strawy pen,
Nor did it occur to one of us there
To doubt they were kneeling then.

So fair a fancy few would weave
In these years! Yet I feel,
If someone said on Christmas Eve,
'Come, see the oxen kneel'

'In the lonely barton by yonder coomb
Our childhood used to know,'
I should go with him in the gloom,
Hoping it might be so.

Thomas Hardy

The Bethlehem Shepherds

I f only we could have been there, Lord,
  on that hillside . . .
We should have heard the sheep baa-ing;
the dogs barking . . .
the silence of the night –
and then, stars –
full of your glory
and the sounds of peace and goodwill . . .
'Glory to God in the highest . . . '

Christopher Herbert

The Kings

L ord, when we bring our gifts to the baby Jesus,
  Help us to give our lives to you –
for you are the true King of the world.

Christopher Herbert

Presents

L ord, may we be thankful for the gift of your
Son, the most important present of all.

Presents

Children of eight and nine years old have very definite views about what makes a good present. A parent, auntie or grandparent who wants to earn the favour of their beloved children should buy a bike, a TV, a CD player, Technic Lego, a piano, a computer, a keyboard, a desk, a hi-fi system, a train set, a watch, a kitten or anything BIG.

If, however, they should dare to produce any of the following, they will definitely be persona non grata: soap and things for the bath, clothes chosen without approval, underclothes, the same thing that was given last year, presents which are too young (or too old), a football shirt for the wrong team and, worst of all, a woolly jumper that itches.

Despite these strong views, when asked what the real meaning of Christmas was, with one voice they cried 'The birth of Jesus in the manger and helping people remember Jesus in case they forget him.' So, deep down, they do appreciate what was the best ever Christmas present.

Children from Cleves School

J o was the first to wake in the grey dawn of Christmas morning. No stockings hung at the fireplace and for a moment she felt as much disappointed as she did long ago when her little sock fell down because it was so crammed with goodies. Then she remembered her mother's promise and slipping her hand under her pillow drew out a little crimson covered book. She knew it very well for it was that beautiful old story of the best life ever lived and Jo felt that it was a true guide book for any pilgrim going the long journey. She woke Meg with a 'Merry Christmas' and bade her see what was under her pillow. A green covered book appeared with the same picture inside and a few words written by their mother which made their one present very precious in their eyes. Presently Beth and Amy woke to rummage and find their little books also – one dove coloured, the other blue; and all sat looking at and talking about them while the East grew rosy with the coming day.

Louisa M Alcott from 'Little Women'

Christmas Parcels

What a coming and a going there has been amongst us Church Mice this Christmas time and what an exchanging of presents. Bertie came to dinner with me on Christmas Day and brought a matchbox full of crackers and what fun we had pulling them and finding out what was inside. Then there were sweets from Lucy, nuts from Aunt Sarah, a very gay tie from Uncle Horace (though I am not sure I shall dare to wear it for it is violet with orange spots). How we admired the wrappings and enjoyed opening all those parcels! 'You know,' said Bertie, as we sat nibbling a piece of cheese from the Rectory, 'these parcels are rather like Church, aren't they?' 'How is that?' I asked, for I couldn't see how they were at all. 'Well,' he went on, 'you have coloured paper and tinsel or ribbon and then you take them away and you find your present inside; in the same way you have a church and hymns and prayers and you look to see what they are wrapping up and you find Jesus – at least you ought to.' 'Well yes,' I said, 'I suppose you do.'

Alec Shearwood

Deborah went off to wrap up her Christmas presents and hide them in a secret place. Teddy Robinson hadn't any presents for anyone, but he was very busy making up a Christmas song which he was going to sing to Deborah on Christmas morning. So far, he had only made up half of it and when he couldn't think of the right words he just sang te-tumty-tum to fill in the spaces. It went something like this:

> 'Hooray, hooray, it's Christmas Day,
> your stocking's full already
> Te-tumty-tum, te-tumty-tum,
> with lots of love from Teddy.'

It's a good idea for a present, he thought, because I don't have to buy it, and I don't have to wrap it up and hide it away; I just make it up in my head and keep it there until Christmas Day. I hope I get it finished in time, he said to himself. At last it was Christmas Eve. When bedtime came Deborah and Teddy Robinson snuggled down together and lay and thought about Christmas until Deborah fell asleep, and then Teddy Robinson lay and thought about Christmas by himself.

Joan G Robinson

The One Gift

We must become accustomed to not seeking or striving for our own interest in anything; rather we should find and grasp God in all things. For there is no gift from God, nor has there ever been, which he gives in order that we might possess it and remain attached to it. Rather all his gifts in heaven and on earth were given solely in order that he could give the one gift, which is the gift of himself. With all the other gifts his only intention is to prepare us for that gift which is himself and all the works he has done in heaven and on earth were done only that he might do the one work that is to be his own delight so that he might be the object of our delight. And so I say: We must learn to see God in all gifts and in all works.

Oliver Davies

Children and Christmas

L ord, help us to approach the manger with
childlike trust, innocence and simplicity.

Children and Christmas _____

Round the manger, every year on Christmas Eve, they gather, a motley band of children in a motley assortment of clothes brought out every December for an annual renovation. Of course, there's always a bit of a battle for Mary's part and countless prima donnas plead to be angels and twirl around in tights and ballet shoes; old surplices or sheets are cut down and decorated with wings and lace. Twisted coat hangers covered with tinsel make halos for children who are far from angelic and the shepherds fight over who will carry the toy lamb. We find more stuffed toys, few of which, it has to be said, bear even a passing resemblance to a sheep; but poetic licence prevails and arguments cease. The Kings look regal in velvet curtains and paste jewellery and carry bubble bath containers and boxes covered in gold paper. And then the children sing 'Away in a Manger', there is a lump in every adult throat and we know that another Christmas has begun.

Hazel Whitehead

Heavenly Father,
at Christmas time, there is so much to enjoy.
Help us never to take things for granted,
to be greedy or selfish
or to forget the needs of others.
Help us to share,
remind us to say thank you
and make our hearts dance
when we think of the gift of your precious son,
the best present of all.
Amen.

Nick Whitehead

O God, our loving Father,
we know the cost to you
of giving us your son.
Help us to give of ourselves
without counting the cost,
to love our friends and neighbours
in the way you love them
and to offer our lives
as a gift for the world. Amen.

Nick Whitehead

Children and Christmas _____

The best things about Christmas are:
  getting presents that you've wanted for ages,
buying presents for other people,
being thanked for the present you gave,
building snowmen and playing snowballs,
decorating the Christmas pudding, and then eating it,
decorating the tree,
going to parties with yummy food,
when all the family comes,
your sister being home from hospital.

Children from Cleves School

Christmas can be a sad time, despite the fun and
  games.
It's sad if:
animals are cold outside,
someone in the family has to work,
there aren't many presents,
people have to spend Christmas on the streets,
you don't get what you wanted,
you get told off for playing with your brother's
    presents,
your Dad has died.

Children from Cleves School

The worst things about Christmas are:
it only comes once a year,
not having a Christmas tree,
the pine needles falling everywhere,
eating too much turkey and Christmas pudding,
someone else getting the present you wanted,
Mum and Dad going shopping and not telling you
    what they've bought,
when your friend goes away and there's nobody to
    play with,
realising you've spent all your money and there are
    still people on your list,
writing all those cards or sending one to somebody
    and not getting one back,
wrapping all the presents and getting stuck to the
    sticky tape,
waking up early but not being able to get up,
having to eat Christmas pudding,
WAITING!
when it is over and you have to take the tree to bits
    and, worst of all,
when you have to go back to school.

Children from Cleves School

Christmas in the Vicarage

There are more bad things I can think of than good things. We're not allowed to open any presents until Dad gets back from saying goodbye to everybody after church which takes ages. And if Christmas Day isn't a Sunday, it feels awkward having to get up for church when you wouldn't usually be going. It gets really tedious singing loads of carols – wherever you go you have to sing 'O come all ye faithful' at the end – at church, in the old peoples homes and sometimes even in assembly. The week before Christmas Mum and Dad are always running around getting things ready and it's annoying when you've just gone to bed and got to sleep and people ring the doorbell and wake you up. That happens all the time, not just at Christmas, but it's worse on Christmas Eve because it takes a long time to get to sleep in the first place and you know it will take a long time to get back again. There are some good things but I can't think of many – there isn't time to be bored and we do get presents from parishioners which we wouldn't get otherwise.

Jonathan Whitehead, aged 10

A Blessing for Christmas Candles

God bless all Christmas candles
wherever they may be:
The rainbow coloured candles
upon the Christmas tree;
The Children's Corner candles
aglow beneath a star,
The love illumined candles
child fixed in painted jar.
The candles in the churches
with haloes round their heads;
the nightlight kind of candle
that friendly comfort sheds.
God bless all Christmas candles
wherever their beams shine,
And may they be reminders
of Bethlehem's bright sign.

Hilda Rostron

Children and Christmas

A Special Nativity by Special Children

Of course, the church wasn't built for wheelchairs and the logistics of getting them all in requires a degree of imagination and flexibility. When Mary is wheeled down the centre aisle with Joseph beside her, there really is no room at the inn (or anywhere else for that matter). We start 20 minutes late because 25 children have had to be transported from school in a posse of minibuses but nobody minds and while costumes are proudly donned and sheep strategically placed, the band tunes up. Weeks of effort and patient coaxing are rewarded when Sharon sings the first verse of 'Away in a Manger' by herself, when Russell reads two verses of the Christmas story, looking to his teacher for approval after every word and beaming proudly when his mission is accomplished, and when the choir sings a catchy Christmas number from memory. Every item is applauded and mutual encouragement and appreciation abound. In a world which values success and achievement, it is this play which should take all the prizes.

Hazel Whitehead

Christmas away from home

L ord, we thank you for our families and homes. Help us to remember that even when they are far away from us we are united through your love.

Christmas away from home _____

Christmas at the Police Station

No matter what shift I have to perform, I know that all calls I have to supervise will be very serious or extremely trivial, for who else calls the police on Christmas Day?

The staff at the station make the day as merry as possible but each incident means someone in difficulty or needing help and often the calls are from extremely lonely people. To each call, I will despatch two officers and in most cases they will face a situation complicated by alcohol.

There are nice moments though, and pleasant people to meet and exchange festive greetings with. Tinsel and stars adorn police cars – but the best bit is always going home.

Noel Craggs, Police Sergeant, Battersea Station

Crisis at Christmas

Last year I did a few shifts as a Crisis volunteer. As a nurse, I was posted to the first aid room. The guests seemed to have lost most of their self-esteem and self-respect and the 'gift' we could give was to treat them as people worthy of respect. These men could also say that 'foxes have their holes but I have nowhere to lay my head'. Well, for eleven days, they did.

The rules for volunteers seemed odd but they made sense. If you're giving out throat sweets, only give one. When somebody, in a fit of generosity, gave out two, there was a fight over the second one!

One of the great sights was seeing the mattresses going down each night, rows of volunteers swinging them into place and our guests retiring into something which more than usually resembled comfort.

Annette Williams

Christmas in Hospital

At seven years old being away from home and separated from your family at Christmas is bad enough; being in hospital is worse; being in an isolation hospital with visitors only allowed to speak to you through a glass screen while dressed in masks and gowns is worse still. On top of that, not knowing whether you are dreadfully sick is the pits.

It happened to me and now, many years later, I still remember waking up at night, scared, in a vast room with tall brass beds lit only by blue, flaring gas lamps. I still remember the kindness shown by the ladies in the ward who knew how scared I was and comforted me. I remember most the sadness when I was told I couldn't take my presents home because of the risk of carrying infection – and the great joy when I discovered Father Christmas had brought two of everything and left one set at the hospital and one at home!

Ian Rose

Christmas Day in the Desert

Our battalion was in North Africa under Montgomery, clearing out snipers in the villages of Syrte and El Agheila. Christmas Eve was reasonably quiet but on Christmas morning we were shelled unmercifully. And then it happened. Andy, a little ahead of me, was hit by shrapnel. Both Andy's legs seemed to have been blasted from his body. As I cradled him in my arms his eyes were fixed, his lips moved and I heard him say, 'Don't leave me.' Then he died. I cried.

Moments later, I felt a tap on my shoulder and looked up into the face of our Padre. Beneath his steel helmet, his face, encrusted with sweat and sand, had a calmness. In a soft voice he said, 'There's nothing more you can do.' As we crawled forward seeking the shelter of a tank, he said to me, 'Come on, let's go home.' I swear there was a twinkle in his eye and a grin on his face, or did I imagine it? Next day, he too was killed and went to his last home.

Bernard Camp

Christmas for a Choral Scholar

Early Christmas morning we gather in the song school to rehearse for the Communion service. Then we process into the cathedral for the worship. Tired voices are given a new lease of life in the knowledge that we are celebrating our Lord's birthday. There is little time for lunch before another rehearsal and Festal Evensong. Then some of the choral scholars prepare a traditional Christmas dinner – which is eventually served at 9.00 pm.

Boxing Day sees the same pattern – rehearsal, Communion but with the added bonus of sherry with the Precentor and lunch with the Bishop. Another practice before the final Evensong which has at least a guaranteed congregation of choristers' parents.

Afterwards, we all travel home for a second celebration of Christmas with families and friends. But it has been wonderful to celebrate Christmas at the cathedral.

Nick Ash

Christmas in Madrid

As the years go by, one Christmas seems like any other but one stands out in my mind, my first in a strange country. I recall the company dinner, without my wife, trying to follow the increasingly rapid foreign conversations. I wondered if life could get worse and just what I was doing there alone, at that time of all times, away from my own home. The worst thing was walking into the Plaza Mayor, the square in the heart of old Madrid, in the cool evening dusk just as the street lights came on. In the middle of the square, all around the statue of Phillip III on horseback (NOT a good king) were rows of kiosks selling little figures for nativity scenes. Dazzling collections of Roman soldiers, shepherds warming themselves by fires, models of Bethlehem-la-Mancha with eighteenth-century innkeepers turning away the village maiden, Mary. Seeing small children with their parents, bright faces reflecting the light of the stalls reminded me of what Christmas is about and who it is for, wherever we are, at home or abroad.

Peter Duffy

Letter from Prison –
December 17th, 1943

From the Christian point of view, there is no special problem about Christmas in a prison cell. For many people in this building, it will probably be a more sincere and genuine occasion than in places where nothing but the name is kept. That misery, suffering, poverty, loneliness, helplessness and guilt mean something quite different in the eyes of God from what they mean in the judgement of man, that God will approach where men turn away, that Christ was born in a stable because there was no room for him in the inn – these are things that a prisoner can understand better than other people; for him they really are glad tidings and that faith gives him a part in the communion of saints, a Christian fellowship breaking the bounds of time and space and reducing the months of confinement here to insignificance. On Christmas Eve I shall be thinking of you all very much and I want you to believe that I too shall have a few really happy hours, and that I am certainly not allowing my troubles to get the better of me. It will be hardest for Maria.

Christmas away from home

It would be marvellous to know that she was with you. But it will be better for her if she's at home. It's only when one thinks of the terrible times that so many people in Berlin have been through lately that one realises how much we have to be thankful for. No doubt it will be a very quiet Christmas everywhere and the children will remember it for a long time to come. But it may perhaps bring home to some people for the first time what Christmas really is. Much love to the family, the children and all our friends. God bless us all.

Dietrich Bonhoeffer

A Lakeside Christmas in Italy

Joseph and Mary, teeth chattering, ferried by floodlight down a wintry, windswept stream. A crib bobbing on Lake Garda. Cribs everywhere, including the railway station with model trains whirring round. Comet tailed stars of Bethlehem in lights. A vast star in white steel, its rays exploding in a Verona square, its 100 foot tail over arching the arena.

Midnight Mass in a packed church, scarlet with poinsettias. Enter Israelites, Romans, the Holy Family and an oversized, pink, plastic baby, arms and legs pointing heavenward. The band strikes up 'Once in Royal'. Should we sing in Italian or English? Neither, for only the choir sings. Pity. We think of England. Some relief when we are all allowed to sing the final carol.

Christmas Day, bright and blue. Lakeside walk, welcoming restaurant, mouth-watering lunch. And not a turkey in sight.

Bernard Day

Christmas at the Hospice

Christmas at the Hospice is
the faces of the dying as they listen to the sound
   of Christmas carols drifting through the building,
the hush of the ward at midnight on Christmas Eve,
   being without pain,
the narrow line between laughing and crying,
being aware that Bill's bed is empty on Christmas
   morning,
the things that are left unsaid,
twinkling lights and a Christmas stocking full of
   surprises on the end of each bed,
a sense of humour,
a card from an old friend, and memories,
staying well enough for the family to visit,
'Happy Christmas, Grandpa'
family being there, or not
friends being there
being loved and accepted and cared about
being given hope and feeling safe and wondering
   if . . .
saying 'Yes' and being thankful.
Wendy Duffy

Christmas away from home ————

Heavenly Father,
it is hard to be away from home at any time
but especially at Christmas.
Be with all our friends who are far away
and keep them safe from harm.
Be with all who are lonely, or in danger,
with all who must work for our benefit
and with those for whom time will hang heavy.
When we are depressed, remind us that nothing
can separate us or our loved ones from your love.
Amen.

Hazel Whitehead

O God, our heavenly Father,
you created families
for our support and enjoyment.
Be with all those families who live with discord,
where violence and bitterness is commonplace.
Bring something of your light into their lives
this Christmas time. Amen.

Hazel Whitehead

Christmas around the world

Lord, we thank you that Christmas is celebrated throughout the world. We pray that one day all will welcome the birth of your Son.

H eavenly Father,
you made the world and all the countries in it,
from arctic pole to tropical forest;
you made all people to enjoy the world
black, white, yellow and brown;
you were born a Jew and yet you died for all people.
Help us to respect the traditions and customs of
those who live in different countries from our own,
because we are all your people. Amen.

Hazel Whitehead

Christmas in Australia

H eat, T-shirts and shorts, cold turkey and ham,
cool watermelon eaten in the shade of the gum
tree in the backyard, sand in our clothes from the
beach picnic, sunburn, midnight service to beat the
daytime heat and crowds, Christmas trees made from
eucalyptus branches and Father Christmas very hot
and sweaty under his red suit, a long swim in the
pool . . . these are the images evoked by the thoughts
of Christmas in Australia.

Doug and Dallas Buckley

A Year in Provence

There was no doubt about the most important ingredient in a Provençal Christmas. Judging by the window displays, the queues and the money changing hands, clothes and toys and stereo equipment and baubles were of incidental importance; the main event of Christmas was food. Oysters and crayfish and pheasant and hare, pâtés and cheeses, hams and capons, gateaux and pink champagne – after a morning spent looking at it all we were suffering from visual indigestion. With our tree and our mistletoe and our dose of Christmas spirit, we came home.

Peter Mayle

Christmas around the world _____

December now was spent in lively dazzly Dublin. Joseph travelled in and out of the city on the train. His dad hurtled along bringing his son all the magic and music, hullabaloo and razzamatazz of Christmas in the capital of Ireland. The crowds made way for the boy in the wheelchair, the waitresses put extra cream in his coffee, the shopkeepers beautifully looked pleased with his choice of presents, while the porters helped him board his train at the vantage point for him. For lonely youth he gave not a fig, here he was now watching people's faces, smiling at times as street dealers raucously bellowed 'Buy your Christmas wrapping paper . . . Lovely balloons . . . Christmas decorations . . . Get your fairy lights . . . Look son, lovely Christmas crackers . . . last two boxes.' Never offended if passed by they just revved up and bellowed again. Seeing but not believing the boy loved the burly busy streets. Great chains of fairy lights mimicked magic for his lost chances.

Christopher Nolan

Christmas in Argentina

For Mataco Indians of the Chaco region of northern Argentina, Christmas occurs at the hottest time of the year. Carol services in mud brick village churches are held at dawn, before it gets too warm. They sing in both Spanish and Mataco to tunes English people would recognise, whilst nearby men oversee the roasting of a whole cow, trying in vain to keep hungry dogs away. After the feast of meat, sweetcorn and rice come the games – egg and spoon and sack races and the pensioners' race – their unlikely prize the head of the cow that fed the whole community.

Dick and Jen Hines

Christmas Day in Kuwait

The sun rises and the temperature is like a warm, spring day. Wild parrots squabble and their calls mingle with the waking of the daily bustle of a capital city, including the call to prayer. The smell of fresh coffee and murmurs of voices herald a new working day. The radio provides a mixture of programmes – from classical music to the local language extolling the activities of the Amir. Although it is Sunday and 25th December, a day's work is obligatory. Treasures such as jars of mincemeat, sausages and bacon, tapes of carols, decorations and crackers, bought on holiday in the summer, rend a simulation of Christmas Day in England. Presents break down all barriers of creed or race and render that glorious feeling of goodwill amongst all peoples. The World Service brings the Queen's Speech into our home and the silver tree and lights cast shadows of memories of friends and Christmases past.

Margaret Klat

Christmas in India

One month before, on November 25th, we celebrate 'suppose Christmas' or 'soon-coming Christmas'. We gather at the church in the evening. 'Let's have a budgenai (carol sing) round the roads where Hindus and Muslims as well as Christians live.' On the back seat of a bike the harmonium is tied; an oil lamp carried on the head provides light; cymbals too help keep us all together. We sing of the coming One, the Light of the world. Let's do a Christmas play, before the holiday: for children in the schools, women in their groups, nurses at the hospital, village people too. Saris are used for dressing up as kings and angels, towels for the shepherds' heads, a real charcoal fire, a real donkey, real lambs, maybe a real, new baby – easily obtained and they add to the drama. Plenty of real stars in the sky above. Christmas is a good time for such activities, weather settled, no rain and not at all cold. Crowds come to an open space, happily they sit and listen as the Christmas story is told.

Audrey Chalkley

Wigilia – A Polish Christmas Eve

When the first star appears on Christmas Eve, the Christmas wafer bread, the oplatek, is broken and shared. All greet each other with a kiss of peace.

The table is laid with a place for the stranger who may come seeking shelter. Hay under the table cloth recalls the manger.

It is the last day of the Advent fast, so no meat is served. Fish in aspic, barszcz with uszki, ravioli style dumplings shaped into 'crowns' for the three kings, then more fish. In the past, twelve fish or twelve courses were served, for Jesus and the disciples. And after the fish, aromatic winter puddings with dried fruit, spices, poppyseed, carroway, sweet noodles and cheesecake.

Then through the cold night air we go to welcome the Christ Child at Midnight Mass.

Irena Czerniawska Edgcumbe

A Norwegian Christmas

Christmas in Norway is celebrated on Christmas Eve, 24th December, with as many family members present as possible. Everyone is dressed up in their best clothes and the festival begins with a visit to church to hear the story of Jesus' birth and to join in singing Christmas carols.

Then it's home through the snow for a traditional dinner – pork, lamb, turkey or fish depending on what part of the country you come from. The dessert is a rice pudding with everyone eager to find the hidden almond, for the lucky finder receives a marzipan ring.

Santa Claus comes shortly after dinner and hands out the presents. Before going to bed, the children hang up their stockings and, if they are lucky, will find them full of sweets on Christmas Day.

Anne Pedersen and Anne Njoten

Christmas in former Yugoslavia

L iving in the iron grip of a communist government meant that although faith was alive in people's hearts, we had to wear dark coats and cover our faces when we went anywhere near a church. Christmas was a particularly difficult time – a time for families to gather close, curtains pulled tight against prying eyes. But one could see, wandering after dark, the flickering lights of many candles and would be comforted by the knowledge that God was still worshipped. Everything about Christmas was a whisper – never a loud song of joy.

When I left school as usual on Christmas Day – for, of course, it was not a public holiday – I was careful, even at that tender age, not to reveal too much and to be careful whom I spoke to. I shall never forget the humiliation I suffered on one occasion, having been given a tiny gold cross on a chain as a present. It was a grammar school and we were expected to conform so I wore my cross underneath my collar, safely tucked away.

As I leaned forward to write in my book it was revealed. My teacher noticed and took it upon herself to humiliate me. I became the focus of attention with the shame of being different. The shame of having a faith I dared to proclaim.

Although I didn't have a job to lose and my family weren't in the Party, we had to go secretly to Midnight Mass, treading an icy path through the snow, only to arrive at a church packed with the faithful, most of whom were from the country where traditional values could be better hidden from the prying eyes of the state. Since its secession in 1989 Slovenia has become an independent republic with religion, at least on paper, officially tolerated and religious holidays respected. But the scarring that we endured as children by daring to be seen at Mass, by believing, was to remain with me.

Majda Gilding

Christmas around the world _____

Christmas in South Africa was in high summer – a time of cloudless, blue skies and sunshine. It was strange attending the Carol Service and Nativity Play in shirts and shorts, then dashing home for a dip in the pool. In the morning we went to church as usual but because it was Christmas our black maid, Josephine, was allowed to come too rather than attending a separate service later in the day – a rare privilege. Being true 'Brits', one thing never changed: we ate our traditional Christmas lunch as we had always done – at lunchtime – even though it was 90 degrees in the shade! Our South African friends thought we were mad as we tucked into turkey and trimmings with customary gusto as the sun blazed overhead and perspiration trickled down our faces. Armies of mosquitos, eager to partake of us and our delights joined us. 'Mad dogs and Englishmen' springs to mind. But undaunted, we upheld our British traditions and then stretched out lazily to enjoy a shady siesta in the warmth of an African Christmas afternoon.

Jenny Chandler

General

Lord, thank you for Christmas and all that it
means to us.

Going the Rounds

The singing boys arrived at the tranter's house, which was invariably the place of meeting and preparations were made for the start. The older men and musicians wore thick coats, with stiff perpendicular collars and coloured handkerchiefs wound round and round the neck till the end came to hand, over which they just showed their ears and noses like people looking over a wall. The remainder, stalwart ruddy men and boys, were dressed mainly in snow-white smock-frocks, embroidered upon the shoulders and breasts in ornamental forms of hearts, diamonds and zig zags. The cider mug was emptied for the ninth time, the music books were arranged and the pieces finally decided upon. The boys in the meantime put the old horn lanterns in order, cut candles into short lengths to fit the lanterns; and a thin fleece of snow having a-fallen since the early part of the evening, those who had no leggings went to the stable and wound wisps of hay round their ankles to keep the insidious flakes from the interior of their boots.

Thomas Hardy from 'Under The Greenwood Tree'

It was a pretty sight and a seasonable one that met their eyes when they flung the door open. In the forecourt, lit by the dim rays of a horn lantern, some eight or ten field mice stood in a semicircle, red worsted comforters round their throats, their forepaws thrust deep into their pockets, their feet jigging for warmth. With bright beady eyes they glanced shyly at each other, sniggering a little, sniffing and applying coat sleeves a good deal. As the door opened one of the elder ones that carried the lantern was just saying, 'Now then, one, two, three,' and forthwith their shrill little voices uprose on the air, singing one of the old-time carols that their forefathers composed in fields that were fallow and held by frost, or when snowbound in chimney corners and handed down to be sung in the miry street to lamplit windows at Yule time.

Kenneth Grahame from 'The Wind in the Willows'

Friday, December 25th, 1942

At 3 pm, after a round-the-world programme, the King broadcast a Christmas message very strongly and clearly, seeming much less nervous. He is, alas, now one with those who mourn someone near and dear in the loss of the Duke of Kent this year. We stood for 'God save the King' and even tried to sing it. All the time we had Nevill and Alan in our minds and hearts, and the King spoke of the thoughts of the Queen and himself being with those 'who have lost their dear ones, those wounded and in hospital . . . the prisoners of war who bear their long exile with dignity and fortitude.'

Mrs Milburn

Christmas Day Alone

I spent the day completely alone. Yes, I could have gone to my sister-in-law and I didn't let the neighbours know in case they asked me to join them out of pity. I went to a 7 o'clock Communion Service and called in on a friend and had a coffee. When I got home I went through cards and so on and then I laid the table and decorated it and lit the candles. Then I cooked beef and trimmings and a small pudding and mincepie – everything. I washed up, sat down. And suddenly laughed. But I didn't mind. I was being cared for. I was happy. I was alone but not alone. I was free of being beholden to anyone. I felt the loneliness of the world was the world Christ came to live in and share. I thought about realities and not escapes. Yes, I was genuinely happy. I listened to carols over and over again and entered the wonderful words, music and inspiration. Perhaps I won't do this again but I shall never be afraid of being alone on Christmas Day. It was a sort of achievement.

Anne Shells

General

The moment Scrooge's hand was on the lock, a strange voice called him by his name and bade him enter. He obeyed. It was his own room. There was no doubt about that. But it had undergone a surprising transformation. The walls and ceiling were so hung with living green that it looked a perfect grove; from every part of which, bright, gleaming berries glistened. The crisp leaves of holly, mistletoe and ivy reflected back the light as if so many little mirrors had been scattered there; and such a mighty blaze went roaring up the chimney, as that dull petrification of a hearth had never known in Scrooge's time, or Marley's, or for many and many a winter season gone. Heaped up on the floor, to form a kind of throne were turkeys, geese, game, poultry, brawn, great joints of meat, sucking pigs, long wreaths of sausages, nuts, cherry-cheeked apples, juicy oranges, luscious pears, immense twelfth-cakes and seething bowls of punch, that made the chamber dim with their delicious steam. In easy state upon this couch, there sat a jolly Giant, glorious to see; who bore a glowing torch, in shape not unlike Plenty's horn and held it up, high up, to shed its light on Scrooge as he came peeping round the door. 'Come in,' exclaimed the Ghost. 'Come in and know me better, man.' Scrooge entered timidly and hung his head before the Spirit. He was not the dogged

Scrooge he had been; and though the Spirit's eyes were clear and kind, he did not like to meet them . . .

. . .'A merry Christmas, Bob!' said Scrooge, with an earnestness that could not be mistaken, as he clapped him on the back. 'A merrier Christmas, Bob, my good fellow, than I have given you for many a year. I'll raise your salary and endeavour to assist your struggling family and we will discuss your affairs this very afternoon, Bob. Make up the fires and buy another coal-scuttle before you dot another i, Bob Cratchit.' Scrooge was better than his word. He did it all and infinitely more; and to Tiny Tim, who did not die, he was a second father. He became as good a friend, as good a master and as good a man as the good old city knew.

Charles Dickens

General

Christmas for many is (or should be) a happy and joyous occasion, celebrating the birth of our Lord Jesus Christ. But consider for a moment those suffering a bereavement at Christmas. As well as the trauma of losing a loved one, the holiday brings its own peculiar problems – some administrative departments are closed at local authority offices, the cemetery and crematorium may not be open for a few days and then there is another Bank holiday – New Year and more time lost. If the death took place some time before Christmas it may be possible to rush things through but what if it happens over the festive period? Families must wait a week or more for the funeral, maybe well into the New Year, and by then most of the clergy have disappeared for their post-Christmas break. It's a nightmare, not only for the bereaved, but also for the funeral director who is struggling to provide an efficient service despite the problems. The house may still be festive with tree lights flickering and crackers on the table but in a home when a bereavement has occurred, there will be quite a different feeling

David Leggett

Christmas as a Vicar

'This must be your busiest time' they say. Sometimes it has been frantic but the diary is strangely clear in the very last days; the schools have broken up – the rush of assemblies and plays are at an end – and committees will wait till new year. There is a lull before the final push – Crib service, Midnight, Christmas Day.

How different from the financial world I left. You could be forgiven for thinking that Christmas was a fleeting interruption rather than a major Christian festival – no sooner home on Christmas Eve than back again just three days later to tired decorations in a half-empty office.

Now this celebration of Christ's birth – the God 'who went about among us' is the culmination of weeks of preparation and has become the very centre of my life.

Nick Whitehead

General

We grouped ourselves around the farmhouse porch. The sky cleared and broad streams of stars ran down over the valley and away to Wales. Everything was quiet; everywhere there was the faint crackling silence of the winter night. We started singing and we were all moved by the words and the sudden trueness of our voices. Pure, very clear and breathless we sang 'As Joseph was a-walking he heard an angel sing, This night shall be the birth time of Christ the heavenly king,' and 2000 Christmases became real to us then; the houses, the halls, the places of paradise had all been visited, stars were bright to guide the Kings through the snow; and across the farmyard we could hear the beasts in their stalls. We were given roast apples and hot mince pies, in our nostrils were spices like myrrh and in our wooden box as we headed back for the village there were golden gifts for all.

Laurie Lee

The Christmas Carol Services

'If I sing that carol again, I shall scream. And it's only 14th December.' For contrary to the Church calendar, Christmas actually begins round about 5th December when the first Carol Service takes place. We start with the Old People's Day Centre with lunch thrown in (not literally, of course); then the uniformed organisations of tiny Rainbows and Beavers and bulky adolescents, carrying flags. Various schools add their own particular something with full blown nativities or variety shows worthy of the London Palladium with casts of hundreds. For some reason, a prayer from the Vicar at the end makes everything legal. The Mothers' Union and residential homes for the elderly at least provide mince pies in abundance and the Toddler Club provides mayhem and fun. By the time we get to the Church Carol Service, when it really is almost Christmas, we have done to death all the popular carols and are ready to scream, but the sound of a solo treble singing the first verse of 'Once in Royal' restores faith in the value of the Carol Service.

Hazel Whitehead

General

We pray you, Lord, to purify our hearts
that they may be worthy to become your
dwelling-place.
Let us never fail to find room for you,
but come and abide in us,
that we may also abide in you,
for as at this time you were born into the world for us,
and live and reign, King of kings and Lord of lords,
now and for ever. Amen.

William Temple

Blessings

Christ the Sun of Righteousness shine upon you
and scatter the darkness from before your path;
and the blessing of God almighty,
the Father, the Son and the Holy Spirit,
be upon you and remain with you always. Amen.

The Promise of His Glory

Christ our Lord, to whom kings bowed down in
worship and offered gifts,
reveal to you his glory
and pour upon you the riches of his grace;
and the blessing of God almighty,
the Father, the Son and the Holy Spirit,
be with you for ever. Amen.

The Promise of His Glory

May the joy of the angels,
the eagerness of the shepherds,
the perseverance of the wise men,
the obedience of Joseph and Mary,
and the peace of the Christ child
be yours this Christmas.

The Promise of His Glory

Index of authors and sources

Index of first lines

Acknowledgements

The compilers are very grateful to the following for permission to quote from their works. Every effort has been made to trace the owners of copyright material; the compilers apologise if any inadvertent omission has been made. Information about such omissions should be sent to the publishers who will make full acknowledgement in future editions.

Extracts from the *Book of Common Prayer*, the rights of which are vested in the Crown, are reproduced by permission of the Crown's patentee, Cambridge University Press. *The Alternative Service Book 1980*, *The Promise of His Glory* and *Together for Christmas 3* are copyright © The Central Board of Finance of the Church of England. Extracts are reproduced with permission.

University of Wales Press: extract by Canon A Allchin from *The Furnace and the Fountain*, Ann Griffiths. SPCK: 'Incarnatus Est' from *The Edge of Glory*, David Adam; 'Whatever gifts' from *Beguine Spirituality*, (ed) Fiona Bowie 1989; 'The One Gift' from *The Rhineland Mystics* (trans.) Oliver Davies. Darton Longman and Todd Ltd: extract from *Rule for a New Brother* by Benedictine Priory, 'Regina Pacis' 1973 and 1986. Asset Publications: extract from 'Joseph and the Shepherds' from *The Place Where Socks Go* by Godfrey Rust 1990; 'The Shepherd's Journey' by Cecily Taylor. Iona Community, Glasgow, Scotland (Wild Goose Publications): 'Send us an Angel' from *The Whole Earth Shall Cry Glory* collected prayers of George F Macleod 1985. 'The Bethlehem Shepherds' and 'The Kings' from *Prayers for Children* by Christopher Herbert, National Society/Church House Publishing. 'Christmas Parcels' from *Tales of a Church Mouse* by Alec Shearwood. SCM: 'Letter from Prison – December 17th 1943' from *Letters and Papers from Prison* by Dietrich Bonhoeffer. Hamish Hamilton Ltd: extract from *A Year in Provence* by Peter Mayle. Weidenfeld and Nicolson: extract from *Under the Eye of the Clock* by Christopher Nolan. 'Christmas in India' by Audrey Chalkley. Judy Milburn and Peter Donnelly 1979: extract from *Mrs Milburn's Diaries*. 'Christmas day Alone' by Anne Shells. Chatto and Windus: extract from *Cider with Rosie* by Laurie Lee. Barbara Grant (translator): 'You are the radiant white lily' by Hildegard of Bingen.

THE NATIONAL SOCIETY
A Christian Voice in Education

The National Society (Church of England) for Promoting Religious Education is a charity which supports all those involved in Christian education – teachers and school governors, students and parents, clergy and lay people – with the resources of its RE centres, archives, courses and conferences.

Founded in 1811, the Society was chiefly responsible for setting up the nationwide network of Church schools in England and Wales and still provides legal and administrative advice for headteachers and governors. It now publishes a wide range of books, pamphlets and audio-visual items, and two magazines, *Crosscurrent* and *Together with Children*.

For details of membership of the Society or to receive a copy of our current catalogue please contact:

The National Society,
Church House,
Great Smith Street,
London
SW1P 3NZ
Telephone: 0171-222 1672